WORD BIRD'S CHRISTMAS WORDS

by Jane Belk Moncure
illustrated by Vera Gohman

Created by

THE CHILD'S WORLD

Distributed by CHILDRENS PRESS ®
Chicago, Illinois

CHILDRENS PRESS HARDCOVER EDITION
ISBN 0-516-06574-2

CHILDRENS PRESS PAPERBACK EDITION
ISBN 0-516-46574-0

Library of Congress Cataloging in Publication Data

Moncure, Jane Belk.
   Word Bird's Christmas words.

   (Word house words for early birds)
   Summary: Word Bird puts words about Christmas
in his word house—North Pole, reindeer, candy canes,
stockings, and others.
      1. Vocabulary—Juvenile literature.
2. Christmas—Juvenile literature.   [1. Vocabulary.
2. Christmas]   I. Gohman, Vera Kennedy, 1922-   ill.
II. Title.   III. Series: Moncure, Jane Belk.   Word house
words for early birds.
   PE1449.M527   1987   428.1   86-31666
   ISBN 0-89565-361-3

OCT 21 87

1 2 3 4 5 6 7 8 9 10 11 12 R 95 94 93 92 91 90 89 88 87

WORD BIRD'S
CHRISTMAS WORDS

Word Bird made a...

word house.

"I will put Christmas
words in my house,"
he said.

He put in these words—

letter

North Pole

Santa's workshop

elves

reindeer

sleigh

Santa Claus

Christmas trees

balls

star

candles

carolers

jingle bells

Christmas cookies

candy canes

toy store

wrappings

gifts

Christmas cards

mistletoe

poinsettias

holly

Christmas flowers

stockings

Christmas story

silent night

Merry Christmas

letter

Santa Claus

North Pole

Christmas tree

Santa's workshop

star

elves

candles

reindeer

carolers

sleigh

jingle bells

words with

Word Bird ?

Christmas cookies

candy canes

Christmas flowers

toy store

stockings

gifts

Christmas story

wrappings

silent night

Christmas cards

Merry Christmas

You can make a Christmas word house. You can put Word Bird's words in your house and read them too.

Can you think of other Christmas words to put in your word house?